RAINSTORM OVER THE ALPHABET

Rainstorm over the Alphabet

Poems
1990-2000

Bill Tremblay

Lynx House Press
Portland, Oregon/ Spokane, Washington

ACKNOWLEDGMENTS

Some of the poems in this collection have appeared in the following literary magazines:

"On Blueberry Hill," "An Inmate Looks at Mt. Tippango," and "Incident on Cerillos Road," *High Plains Literary Review*; "Trusting the Music," *Indiana Review*; "Ode for the Sleepless," "Yucatán Dream," and "A Night On the Town," *Green Mountains Review*; "A Front Range Sky" and "Streetlamp," *Ohio Review*; "Learning to Listen," *The Journal* (Ohio State); "The Sagebrush Hours," "A Juniper," "Auto-Surgery" *Willow Springs*; "Frida's Cremation," "Dream of An Afternoon," and "Night Augury," *Spoon River Poetry Review*; "Buried Tenor," *The Bloomsbury Review*; "The Lost Boy," "Huichol Jaguar's Head," "Somnabulist Dawn," and "Blind Side," *Luna*; "No Man's Land," "First Commandment," "Leon's Love Letter to Frida," and "The Music While the Music Lasts," *Manoa: An International Magazine of the Pacific Rim*; "Walking Toward Round Butte," *The Midwest Quarterly*; "Like Father," *Connecticut Poetry Review*; "Church Dream" and "Auto De Fé Dream," *Poet Lore*; "Hollywood Comes to San Angel," *The Massachusetts Review*; "Looking for Inspiration," "The Undead," and "Redbrick Factory Blues," *Heliotrope*; "My Uncle Pete," *turnrow*; "Second Wind," *Upstairs at Duroc*; "Trotsky's Double @ the Moscow Station," *River King*; "Wicked Messenger," "My Parents Before Marriage," "Uses of the Slow Fade," "Tiny Tim As I Remember Him," "American Fable," "Samba on Bass and Alto," "Milkweed Art," "Family Reunion," *Diner*.

Cover and book design by Joelean Copeland
Cover Art by Mary Josephson

Lynx House Press books are distributed by
Small Press Distribution, 1341 Seventh St. Berkeley, CA 94710

Lynx House Press

420 W. 24th Ave.   9305 SE Salmon Ct.
Spokane, WA 99203   Portland, OR 97216

Library of Congress Cataloging-in-Publication Data

Tremblay,   Bill.
    Rainstorm over the alphabet : by Bill Tremblay.
        p. cm.
    ISBN 0-89924-111-5 – ISBN 0-89924-110-7 (alk. paper)
    1. West (U.S.)–Poetry. I. Title.

PS3570.R38 R35 2001
811'.54–dc21

                                                                    2001038807

for Cynthia, love of my life

TABLE OF CONTENTS

Part I

Part II

Part III

Part IV

I

What wakes the music
wakes the muse . . .
—William Ryan
To Die In Latin

STREETLAMP

To be a street lamp
giving off a globe of cold
cadmium light to a *cul-de-sac*
is to make an opening in the sleepless dark
through which comfort pours
like a fountain, inviting those who enter
to imagine underground cables
connecting to the Rawhide Flats power plant
twenty miles north, which turns
black coal into this sentinel
that only wants to shine
on the flat brows of houses
held in the winter murk of what passers-by
feel is locked, yet promising,
a dream that leaves them
reaching into the tense within,
that lets them go past this made
thing of glass and incandescing
wire, this tree of light
with the face of a small god
standing between dusk and dawn,
weary from making another false
day, blotting out the stars
and the darkness inside us.

SOMNABULIST DAWN

I wake to find myself blue
and blanket-wrapped like Chief
Seattle knee-deep in snow
on the Warren Lake spillway.
First light spreads its fungus.
My head steams, my heart
bumps so hard I fall, dizzy, in
wind-whipped wondering what
blizzard has blown me into this
drift where sleet peppers
my one good eye and a sky
the color of my mother's iron hair
demands to know why I have forsook
the faith she hammered into me.
The wind says,
Insomnia is spiritual.
I get to my knees, raise my arms,
addressing the blackboard clouds.
It's not that I've sinned, exactly, I say,
I just have a different aesthetic.
I never liked the old prayers.
and have dreamt all my life
of making new ones.

LOOKING FOR INSPIRATION

With Dada tantrums
do I dose myself, self-ellipsis
lyposuction, freeing all pronouns
to float in the no-intentions æther.
I try therapists for my issues —
the persistent delusion I have a soul,
a rage for the unattainable.
I try sleep deprivation — anything
to subvert the empty page as metaphor —
climb red cliffs above a river, asking
the Muse if she has kissed me off,
forever. The stream sparkles.
Ripples purl the shallow's rock loom.
I crunch across gravel beds grown
savage with gold brush. In tawny grass
I hear dry metal ratcheting like locust wings,
blade on carbon blade. A rattler lifts
its diamond head, cocks its body in an
S. Its scales glow as it shrives off
last year's skin. Garnet beads
twitch with divine telegraphy.
It strikes, blind, cowled. Fangs glint
with clear epiphany: I can't
kill everything that scares me.
Perhaps I should change
my technique. They say if you pierce
your nipples with rings and yank,
the rest of you will follow.

SUMMER OF LOVE

In the beginning was the cliché.
I'm half in the bag all the time,
lubricating my
contradictions. My wife slapped
me for scaring the kids. I asked
a shrink, Which one of me
has the hollow leg? She said
a power suit will hold your self
esteem together. I parked outside
my goldfish bowl gunning my engine
until it screamed bloody murder.
I'm so American, a puritan hedonist!
I shouted, in a fit of self-analysis.
I'll write myself out of this
pickle, use only infinitives, stop
passing the virus. But as I scanned
the words began to divide, divide.
An eraser would not be enough.
I thought. I need a stroke
a rainstorm over the alphabet.

AUTO-SURGERY

As I sleepwalked
late one buttery August
afternoon, dragging my shadow
toward a liquor store,
along the avenue named for the man
who invented strategic bombing
my hands shook, indisputably, with fear
the aortal string where once I plucked
my only song. To save my life
it became necessary to take myself seriously
apart. With a dull barlow knife
I sawed my head from the parts
below. The first victim of my
self preservation was
my voice. Not that I was silent.
No, my windpipe bubbled on, but
there was no longer a first person.
I sat on a stump among inky caps
and cut my legs from their hip
sockets, the ones carrying me
against instinct toward the whiskey
that was killing me. I slashed my
arm from its shoulder until I
was a worm crawling wetly under
lilac bushes back to the bungalow
where my family waited,
through the long boring years for me
to grow new extremities.

THE LOST BOY

Across the Poudre river bridge
stands a stone monument to a lost boy.
Carved words fix the mystery. Did
he wander off, or was he carried off
by tooth or talon? Family, friends,
searched the mountainside calling his
name. The weather turned. Sleet, wind,
snow in slants across the ponderosas.
He blacked out under the canyon's
Milky Way. I hear his cries in
echoing arroyos. Though his bones
mouldered in cold drizzle he comes
crashing through wild plum thickets
clutching at my shirt, asking where I was
in his sagebrush hours. Through his
ripped jacket a flash of bone. I dare not
touch his skeletal shoulder. He's forgotten
how to be alive. The climb is no relief,
his weight dogs my knees. Breezes
sough through purple yarrow aspen groves,
dry waterfalls. I reach the cloud meadows,
hairpin switchbacks until Mount
Greyrock juts its granite forehead into
one hard thought: what remains unfinished
in the soul keeps doubling back
until earth and sky are balanced aches
like the cliff swallow's swift flight.

THE SAGEBRUSH HOURS

— for Bill

You were eight when you walked,
all by yourself, across the dusty road
to the Sagebrush Bar to see what was
in there that made your father prefer
it to you. The backflaps of its louvered
doors knocked you back on your
sitter, and your father like the drunken
cowboys, their handlebar moustaches
dripping golden flecks of beer,
laughed at you. That was when you
got lost as surely as the boy who wandered
off into Poudre canyon's wilderness.
Your father stepped through a door
in time to leave the burden of your life
behind. He stayed until midnight
to hear the Last Train to the Coast Band
play its set, the sax man in porkpie hat,
a syncopated zag of hips in a zoot,
the songbird in her strapless prom dress
lamenting the Night the Music Died.
She was Isis in Lama boots, real
cockroach kickers, her white orchid
no mere knock-off of Lady Day.
The cowboys saw her face as a tin mask.
Put a cork in it! one of them yelled.

Your father was hip to this tableaux,
it was all too typically American,
a jazz band razzed in a cowboy bar.
What he could not see was the rain
that touched everything that night.
You were alone, shivering, ice
forming in your heart
freezing closed
on little hingelike wings.

Iron Mountain

At timberline
beside a hanging lake
tinted the teal isotope of iron
as I look at Long's Peak
butterflies flutter Bach trills
among tundra flowers.
Two elk bound past.
Then as I cross scree fields
granite talus bows out, tilting
my balance so askew I gag,
brain spun with light oxygen
and spider belly-down hand
and foot, spraying debris
into air below, setting off
a childhood memory —
once in the black punishment
corner of my bedroom
when I was nine I saw a Cro Magnon
sitting cross-legged at a cave mouth
in the Pyrennes, gazing down
at a river valley. No longings,
no regrets clouded the membrane
between the sea of grass
and the green sparkle of eyes.

CHURCH DREAM

I told my brother
there was a poet so drunk
another man had to turn his pages.
He said, Let's go inside.
We dipped a knee on the center aisle.
I hadn't forgotten the invisible
line between me and the *sanctum
sanctorum.* The priest rang
the chalice. Maidens danced
to the altar-rail. A St. Francis statue
with a dove on his fingertip
turned and winked at me,
nodding toward the incense
and silky legs spiraling up the nave.
It's all right, he said,
you just have spiritual stage-fright.
My chest was packed. Like a nation
in there. I told my brother,
I walked out on all this —
the sheep, the goats, the wheat, the chaff.
I know, he said,
you made your desk your altar.

ODE FOR THE SLEEPLESS

A flock of geese cries so
loud over checkered roofs
it startles every light sleeper.
Bath-robed, alone, yawning
we put kettles on, asking ourselves,
Why aren't the birds asleep
on the ice, their heads tucked
underwing? We're lost in midnight
questions as if the kitchens
where we stand under Orion's sparkle
never could be home. Yesterday
was different. We walked under huge
abstract skies talking about the gifted ones
who don't love themselves.
We imagined voices pulling them
apart lung from lung until all that's left is
the one who knows how far back
this really goes, who hears
a tangled heart that got that way
long before it learned to speak,
who feels life brimming at the eyes,
who still believes, who keeps dawn
safe, so we can sleep, so we can
dream that night birds
signaling each other in the dark
change what language can be.

II

The mixed messages of childhood: the double binds of adulthood.

No Man's Land

You are five OK who cares, who cares your mother
takes you every morning to a lady's house who takes
care of you near the factory where they manufacture
facts and that day across the cold coalyards you've
already begun to figure out how the world works All
summer railcars railcars dump Pennsylvania coal in
the yards you're crossing waiting waiting for winter when
people burn the coal to keep from freezing in the cold
and the eyeglasses your mother makes in the factory
go out to Pennsylvania to help the miners see But
as you think of sitting alone at Wilhelmina's all day
watching the sky it's like car sickness, this lump of
fact you are swallowing You beg as you cross the coal
yard Don't leave me at Wilhelmina's Your mother
leans over you, her face is giant, Who cares Who
cares what you think! she yells, I have to work!
Your tongue is froze in cold black coal dust
You call up your final courage to ask
how come she says I have to have my own money
or your father...you hear her voice die in the useless
why the inconceivable how From then till now, who
cares if you turned out OK at catching on even if
your hands are sewn on backwards Facts are bigger
than your mother, your invisible father, and you

LIKE FATHER

Kitchen hubbub shakes us from our dreams
We rub our aching eyes
Mother, brothers, sister circle father
his head in skullcap gauze
Somewhere outside Bridgeport
the story goes he's stopped by roadflares
Two hoods pull him from his truck cab at gunpoint
march him to the trailer door, force him to break the seal
What cargo? Eighteen tons of Chesterfields
They blackjack his lights out
When he comes to he's in Emergency
Does it hurt? His head throbs like jazz band bass fiddle
But why you? how did they know?
Can't remember, head hurts, need sleep
We all do, as we lift our knees onto mattresses
As we lie there sleepless dawn lightens windows
We know it's a Mafia heist
We know our father owes them large
We lie there wondering what our future holds
Shivering, we almost lost our dad
We lie there, love and shame like clashing gears
We lie there, praying we're not chips off the old block
We lie there, impossible to say an "Our Father"

WICKED MESSENGER

One summer afternoon
cicadas whine on telephone wires
like a prelude to *petit mal*
gathering in the air outside our
three-decker apartment in Southbridge
There's a knock on the screen door
A blond young man steps into the kitchen
The look on my sister's face means
she feels attraction   Mother in her rocking
chair by the open window hooks yarn
into an afghan   Why won't you admit I'm
your son, he pleads
with sparks in his eyes
It says your name on my birth certificate
Look, she says, rocking herself up
This was all decided in court
He flinches but holds his ground
He looks as if he wouldn't mind if she hit him
Why does she give me that red look?
I am five years old   What is this about?
Why does she let me go to the movies that day?
Does she think I won't ask God that night
if my father is my real father?
Will I be judged at Heaven's Gate
on secrets I've never been told
as if I only half belong?
But God is God and doesn't say

First Commandment

In fourth grade
I wondered why after all his
te deums and *oremuses*
Fr. Smith in white chasuble would chant
"I am the Lord thy God,
thou shalt have no other before me,"
pounding the ark against idolatry.
No pagans danced midnight meringues
with Moloch in my parish.
Then one day my father showed me *The Racing Form*.
I was to perform the miracle of long division
by seconds into furlongs.
Did I see one number glow like a horseshoe in a forge?
I saw hoofs flashing,
wind whistling through a jockey's helmet.
Later, when he drove me to his
place of worship with its flags and roses,
I got his number as he shouted *Whip that horse!*
in the final stretch. He hit the Double,
the goddess smiled on him.
He lifted me on the geyser of his joy.
Then I watched him play the tote board,
sure the changing odds would show him
where the fix was in, over and over
until he was broke and though I choked
on the Eucharist of ripped-up tickets

I saw through that scared look on his face
he wouldn't know who he was
if he came home a winner.

FAMILY REUNION

Amazing how little being right
matters in the world, I observe to my
sister-in-law as we boil in the
outdoor jacuzzi. My brother gives
me a mock back-hand slap to ape
our parents. It's all in the genes, she
claims. You can go mad dieting,
but a mesomorph you will always be.
Self-love means never having to
buy a self-help tape. Pass the sun
block, I say, as I watch derricks
fly girders into Paris,
Las Vegas, dreaming backwards
to childhood when my family
were geniuses of the impossible
edifice of the good life in America.
Build the roof first, then levitate it!
they commanded. Only in dreams
did I ever get it off the ground.
My sister-in-law lolls in steam.
I gaze at my difference in the bubbling
water. How did you keep from
going crazy? she asks. I answer,
Who says I'm not crazy?

My Parents Before Marriage

Thirteen motorbikes on the starting line,
thirteen stories at the county fair,
stars blotted out by klieg-light shine,
gunning their engines for the winner's share,
the flag falls fluttering through summer
night, flying tangled leather legs
all kick back, thirteen racers crank throttle
in fishtail flight, motor roar rooster tail
dirt geyser track, the young man's white
teeth flash beneath dirty goggles, my
father a second base double A Yankee
minor leaguer by day, night-time
racer on a quarter mile course, boxed in,
thinking line-drive snag underhand toss to short,
he drafts on the leader in the final turn,
swings into high for the winner's pole,
his two-lung Bugati pistons burn like flares,
he throws a rod and oil gushes in the dust,
his drive train locks up, he slams a haybale
Twenty feet from the finish line stands
my mother with bobbed black hair,
hand to mouth to stifle a scream.

MY UNCLE PETE

My mother gave him his
nickname, English for *pauvre
pitou*, when he fell in a trash barrel
fire. A schoolboy, I thought
Icarus too close to the sun
when he showed me his web of scars
like a beaten silver breastplate.
How much he could have taught me
I think, remembering his Land
camera, the red glow of his darkroom,
the miracle of negative to positive.
I could've become a photographer,
taking shots all over my home
town. My first big coup,
a thousand suns setting in a thousand
factory windows. Then spangled
sun flecks on leaf tips by the river,
banks of votary candles flickering in
St. Mary's. I see myself asked by
interviewers to explain my first
gallery show. Like my uncle Pete
who lost the power of speech from
the shock of his burns I would
struggle to say I don't believe in
the Sublime but the photos keep
telling me different.

ON BLUEBERRY HILL

I dream my hedge is blown away
by a Siberian wind come loping down
through Canada, the lawn widowed.
A voice says my name. I say, Yes?
even before I open my eyes and find
my lids are two pools of black water.
Is it an angel or the lost boy asking
what first love is like. I show him
the movie. She, driving down a logging
road in her mother's new convertible,
oaks arching over green shadows cast
on moss rocks. He, a young man, lies
back staring into branches laced like
lovers' arms envined. Radio saxophone
breezes, a boom shot above treetops
showing the town, miles away, church
steeples, town hall, clock tower, shops
where store clerks with purple bags
under their eyes like sporting house
blues piano players hit five and dime.
Cessnas sputter offscreen, taxiing on
the runway in sync with cicadas droning
like comb and paper kazoos. What the
movie is all about is the sound track, her
family in steerage from Ireland, his
walking 300 miles from Laurentian farm
valleys to milltown factory jobs. What he

gasps as he kneels between her thighs with
the radio knob throbbing Fats Domino in
his spine is how much he feels the music's
throat-ripping strain his soul can count the
anecdotal beat of in his blood, high-balling
through all the local stops, sha-booming
like a national express. What the music
bruises them with bleeds pink like her chiffon
Isadora Duncan scarf. What he asks her is,
What sense does virtue make if there's no
redemption as great as this salt burn at the
lips of Hell? Her kiss blushes his face,
the wind stands still. Sunlight opens
between his shoulder blades. What she
whispers is, We'll be together in Eternity
as she drops the shift in reverse and backs
them down to their betrayals. The smile he
thought would always get him up she
gives to someone else. He doesn't marry
her. He marries the one he can grow up
and have children with. Yet his life
turns into one held breath, a dream he
wakes from one morning to find black
water standing in the wells of his eyes.

MILKWEED ART

When Indian summer
painted the oak vermillion
and the sky was afloat with white-topped
gray-soled sandals of old gods
air drunk with juice of apple falls
I used to see them, stands of them,
grown sere along the leaf-choked river
with pods the size of tanagers
clinging to autumn stalks.
It wasn't against nature
to jump the gun before November
winds harked slant snow, to break open
their husks that just fit a child's hand
until I could see the brown seeds
packed inside long white shiny
feathers, to send them flying
with a quick backward
flick of the wrist, to make them
billow on breezes like swarms of galleons.
My wife's father would wait, though,
until they were brittle, empty,
to glue little felt ears on their half-shells
and tan yarn tails and beads
that turned them into black-eyed mice
to hang on the Christmas tree.

III

. . . not only bread but poetry.
— Leon Trotsky,
"To the Memory of Essenin"

LETTER TO FELIPE GARRISÓN

I took Cynthia to see everything you
showed me. We stood before the rain
god's statue. I told her how they dug it
up in Oaxaca and shipped it on a flatbed
railcar to Mexico City, and cloudbursts
shook each pueblo Tlaloc traveled through.
I could see the power continue as her gaze
went inside where the lightning lives.
Everyone I ask remembers the Angel of
Independence falling from her pedestal in
the storm but not the suicide note in her
hand. I believed you. Like Diego I believe
everything. We got aboard a boat called
Xochimilco crowded on a grand canal,
families, big picnics, beer and ice. Jan said,
They've grown flowers here a thousand years.
You mean we're on one of *the* canals? A
mariachi band floated up, *Voy a tocar una
canción para su sombrero pequeño*, the
trumpet player said. When I reached down
to cup some water to splash my face I saw
fifty naked plastic dolls crucified on a wire
fence. An old woman paddled up in a rose
canoe. *Viente cinco*, she said *No entiendo*,
John replied, *Cuál lengua hable? Americano*,
she laughed, her gold tooth glinting. I put
the roses in water back at the hotel so they'd

keep longer. I tried to understand the Mexican
attitude toward death. The closest I come
is: when we die we nourish the living. But
everything keeps blooming in Cynthia's eyes.

Yucatán Dream

I ride all day beneath clouds
towering heron-white
infinite with spaces leading
my eye onward into

the furthest blue. That night
in Merida I dream of standing
on my Aunt Lil's balcony looking
out at the small park where

Uncle Bill taught me to ride
my first bicycle. A Yucatán sky
curves like a hall of bouganvillea
above my home town elms and

a daytime star tells me
in silver pulses I translate
by the skin of my teeth por
milagro in phrasebook Spanish.

Impressionist Show at the Bellas Artes

Art deco zinc lilies,
stalks of maize, one poppy
in a wheat field inside lava walls
a redhead's halo tints her forehead
beaks of white birds eat marble columns
Cuahtemoc runs toward Cuernavaca
holding out the bloody stumps of his severed
hands as proof of Cortez's intentions
Rivera paints with a brush
Siqueiros with a blow-torch
A woman paints a woman painting a woman
lost in a book where she becomes the rust
of exhaustion on a ballerina's lips,
the downcast eyes of winter trees
civilization and all its denizens with cool eyes
after two thousand years of longing for God
and the passer-by locks in for a moment
postponing this fate, fascinated, stopping to see
the art of despair called uncertainty,
the poignancy of solid things
like Diego's skinny dog
who waits for the boy to fall sleep
before snatching his taco, vanishing,
leaving us with nothing, no one,
only colored flecks always about to fly off,
only androgynous children
in the thick velvet curtain shadows
of a Victorian house that has eaten the light

Huichol Jaguar's Head

Beads, one by one, in a matrix of warm beeswax
the ears like fletched rainbow palmfronds
the better to hear you with
the vaudeville proscenium of its mouth
its winking smile like a red *diablo* strangling a bug-eyed *taxista*
the ark of animals, two by two,
the curling antennae of its spectral dragonflies
the yellow radiance of their navels
the white wings of its eye teeth
the gaslights of its lower jaw
the rabbits with black eyes like salivary glands
the redbrick road of its tongue stippled with poppies
open prayer of its sunset throat
        filled with cricket song and castanets
the drunk with mescal skin snoring under the roof of its mouth
the golden jaw like the body armor of your mother's sorrow
the orange spreading nova of its nostrils
the black hexagons of its cathode eyes
the better to see you with
the twin scorpions of its forebrain, stingers poised like the final q
the galaxy of its skull, spiral serpents hissing
the jaguar's head, its bi-lateral symmetry
the peyote button of its chin
the beautiful kitty

TROTSKY'S DOUBLE @ MOSCOW STATION

When Zinoviev tapped his watch
I stepped on the Pullman's landing.
Its small proscenium cowled my head.
I gazed at the pillar of steam
as if taking a last look at a beloved.
My chest swelled on gauze wings.
True, I was a quick study, but this was
improvisation. I seized upon trains.
It had always been trains with him,
the Finland Station where it all began,
the icy years of civil war chugging
from battle to battle beneath the silent
Urals. I raised my hands to calm the crowd.
I am at peace, I said, with my fate.
Someone in the crowd cried, *Don't
leave us!* I'm not leaving, but carrying
the permanent revolution forward. *When
will you return?* another shouted. Perhaps
never, I said, for what we face when we fight
for a better future is not a tyrant's howitzers
but contentment with past victory,
as a poet might rest in the arms of his
last good metaphor, as surprising as seeing
his son kiss his boyfriend for the first time,
a spiritual sleep, while the thing that lives

inside the words has fled. In that moment,
I became Trotsky. *Good work,* Zinoviev
whispered, *you have given them
a vain dream to waste their lives on.*

NIGHT AUGURY

Frida limps under a guarter moon
through the bamboo garden She stands
before the replica of an Aztec altar,
lights a torch, splits the rind of darkness open
Ochre masks, jaguars, serpents
In a glyph a king pierces his foreskin
with a bone knife and single drops of rain
spatter on dry azalea leaves
She unfolds a newspaper photo
The young Trotsky stands on the Kremlin balcony
Lenin's sponsoring hand on his shoulder
In Red Square millions march to celebrate the first May Day
She unwraps her gauzed foot
Thick clots glop onto the newsprint
She feeds the spattered picture to the flame
A little girl with jade eyes approaches her
from palmetto frond shadows
What of the exile? Frida asks her
The girl holds out a straw basket, one large leathery egg
Frida breaks it open
A baby crocodile squirms out of clear glistening jelly
It bites her thumb, then springs away,
under magnolia bushes
Frida watches blood pool in her palm
A red star

Dream of an Afternoon

Trotsky unlocks the studio,
its door creaks open, sunbeams streak down,
skylight dust rises from under his feet
in swirling puffs — pinned to a wall,
sketches for a mural —
the artist as a boy surrounded by his ghosts,
Mexico's ghosts, real and legendary —
"La Caterina" the grinning skeleton woman
her skull festooned with ostrich plumes
clavicles draped with a feather boa —
Trotsky smiles as he sees
Diego has painted as a boa constrictor skeleton
Then he is deawn to Frieda's eyes
as she holds a black and white Taoist cueball
two fishes in a frozen spiral her eyes
stare out to the future he imagines is him
waltzing her into the air above the fountains
above feathery pastel pink elm tree leaves
above Diego's dead revolutionaries, Aztec
chiefs, Conquistadors, Hidalgo in priest collar,
Morelos's bandana head, Santa Ana,
saintly Benito Juarez   The wall is full of blood
Madero murdered, Zapata murdered,
Carranza murdered, Huerta exiled, death
without certificate Trotsky's fingers tremble
above Frida's painted lips He envies
the sunlight that touches her

HOLLYWOOD COMES TO SAN ANGEL

Diego jams a champagne bottle
like maracas in a silver ice bucket.
Campesinos march, machettes on shoulders, on his walls.
The doorbell chimes. When he opens,
there stands Paulette Goddard, a small woman
in a big garden-party hat. She hands him an envelope,
"From Gershwin," she says.
"What are you doing in Mexico?" He rips the letter open.
"A photo-shoot for *Look* magazine
to publicize my latest comedy . . .
and I want you to paint my portrait."
Diego reads. "He calls me a 'latin lover'?"
"Aren't you?" Paulette's eyes twinkle.
"The virility of the men in my family is a curse."
"Just my luck," she says, unpinning her hat.
"But how shall I pose you?"
Paulette's eyes say she will become whatever Diego imagines.
He backs her toward a wall covered in photographer's backdrop paper.
"Was that a tango?" she asks, staring up.
Diego feels her heat, her small intakes of breath.
"The Hollywood screen has never done you justice," he says.
"You like the movies?" she picks up the champagne.
"The gangster movies, the slang they talk, it tickles me."
"Say some," she says, peeling back the pink foil.
"You have a European kisser," he says like Edward G. Robinson.
"I'm American, pure mongrel, half Jewish."
"Me too," he says, "I trace back to a mystic philosopher from Lisbon."

"Stop, you're making me nervous," she laughs.

"How is Mexico treating you?"

"Fine, except at the bullfight, the matador gave me the tail,

but some jerk said the bull-fighter was an amateur.

I said, 'Maybe, but the bull's a professional.'"

The tip of her tongue between her teeth as she untwists the wires.

He settles Paulette down on pillows.

"Now what?" she asks, looking at his zipper.

"Now we wait for the magic. Did you know I was raised by a *bruja*?

You see, my twin brother Carlito died at one year old.

My mother fell upon his grave, wouldn't leave the cemetery.

My father rented her a room in the caretaker's house.

He sent me to Antonia while he struggled for my mother's sanity.

"So you have two mothers, and one is a witch?"

"A *curendera*. When I arrived I didn't have much will to live."

"Understandable," Paulette says, "Your real mother was . . . grieving.'

"Antonia had a plan. She convinced a goat to suckle me."

Paulette looks up, dumbstruck, awestruck.

"I'm more animal than man," he laughs.

She gets up to give him a kiss, but he pulls back.

"Don't you like me?" she pouts.

"It's hard for a man whose mother was a goat to take himself seriously."

"You and Frida are getting a divorce, right?"

"Alas," he sighs.

As Diego leans to kiss her, Paulette shrieks.

Frida's pet monkey, Fulang, has jumped on her shoulder.

"I've had rivals in love, but that . . ."

". . . You move me," Diego interrupts, "like the inherent beauty of . . ."

"Aw, shucks, Diego," she interrupts back,

looking for something to change the subject to.

"What about that?" she asks.

A charcoal sketch on the wall shows a pig-nose general
dancing with a donkey-head politician.

"Where are you in the picture?"

Diego points to a grinning skull with the word *Eternidad* on its
forehead.

"Mio Dio!" he cries, "I was supposed to meet Trotsky!"

"*The* Trotsky? When?"

"Five. Is it five?"

"I'll tell you a secret that works with cars.

You hit the gas, never the brakes, you hold your breath, and you get
there . . .

Hey!" Paulette calls out, as Diego heads for the door.

He returns, snatches her up in his arms.

She reaches down to the bulge in his pants.

"*O my*," she whispers.

LEON'S LOVE LETTER TO FRIDA

When I saw you against the sky climbing
the Sun Temple in the City of the Gods I
glimpsed your divinity   Perhaps it is Mexico,
perhaps it is the heat that dissolves my brain
as shimmering air dissolves the walls of your
Blue House where I live like a man obsessed
No one since Alexandra has stirred such
tender passion in me   She was the bravest
woman I ever loved   We were revolutionaries
together exiled to Ust-Kut in a tarpaper shack
between the forest and the Lena River   At
night when we looked at one another with love
eyes we had first to shut out the screams of
drunks from the saloon next door and then
pinch the light from our candle to lie
in the dark, bedeviled by cockroaches crawling
over our naked bodies alone in the Siberian
winter, our cries answered by wolves
                    We made two little
girls together — one who died years ago, one
who took her life it seems only yesterday
rather than face torture in Stalin's dungeons —
We stayed sane because we were young
and because we read Marx to each other
during those fifty below zero nights, happy
to have even one potato to make a thin soup,
dreaming of escape to London to join Lenin,

to write for the Bolshevik newspaper, *Iskra,*
which means "the spark" in English, the
language I must use here since you don't
have Russian, I don't have Spanish She sent
me away when my chance came, "You must,"
she whispered as we held each other one last
time Yet I remember her eyes with such
regret I don't want to make that mistake
again, Frida

       My marriage to Natalia is
how shall I say You should see us alone
together We have nothing left between us
but our sons Not a word passes She
withdraws to her room, I to mine   though
in public she pushes me to keep faith with
the myth of "the Opposition" How crazy
I must sound, weighing a life of struggle
for justice against the slim chance of finding
happiness with you Don't think I haven't
heard you say, "I tire of *el viejo*" I have enough
Spanish to know that It's the truth I am
sixty years old, and you but half my age
I know it's no way to woo a woman to speak
of loving another years ago I know it's
not wise to complain of one's empty
marriage So bourgeois I shake with shame
If you reject me again I will tell myself
that as I love you I should leave you alone
People close to me turn up dead

Yet I find myself sitting
here melting in this August afternoon in
the invisible ink of my sweat writing words
utterly alien to me, words about your lush
green garden as the Eden Alexandra and I
once imagined, the beautiful future that
I think now will find its completion only
long after my death   I feel as if I have died
already, as if I have already given my life
to my ideals and the fires of my October
have spent themselves in ash   Yet with
the last ember of my soul I dream of you
and I on the coast near Tehuantepec, you
painting, I writing, both of us at last finding
the peace we long for to create   Am I mad
If so, I embrace this dream of embracing
you till death and the tides shall cease

A Night on the Town [mexico city, 1938]

In "The Cockatoo" the orchestra is a forest of gleaming brass
Their lapels reflect sparkles from the mirror ball.
The bandleader conducts with his clarinet.
A willowy blond and her escort sit at a second-row table.
Dance with me, Frank, she begs.
The singer steps up to the microphone.

> *In olden times a glimpse of stocking*
> *was looked on as something shocking*
> *now Heaven knows, anything goes*

Half the trombonists swing the barrels of their horns sideways.
Half bend at the waist and just miss being hit.
Dancers spin in flecks of light.
Frank watches Diego, Frida, Trotsky, Natalia, Paulette Goddard at their table.
Diego and Frida walk to the dance floor.
She wears a polished obsidian tuxedo and moves without a limp.
Come on! Sylvia says.

> *The world's gone mad today*
> *and good's bad today*
> *and most guys today*
> *that women prize today*
> *are just silly gigolos*

Frank watches as Trotsky cuts in on Diego.
Diego pouts as he slouches back to his table.
It's the old man's night to howl, Sylvia says.
They're all fossils, Frank sneers, relics of the previous century.
He dances Sylvia toward Frida, close enough to eavesdrop,
close enough to slash the old man's throat.

I'm under your spell, Trotsky's saying.

Frida puts her hand on his chest and pushes him away.

It's over, she says, whatever there was.

Frank watches Frida leave Trotsky standing there.

She goes to Paulette, holding out her hand.

Paulette rises, looking back at Diego.

The songbird steps to the microphone.

> *Some times I wonder why I spend*
> *the lonely night, dreaming of a song . . .*

Frida presses Paulette to her tuxedo.

You're so strong, Paulette says.

I'm relentless, Frida says, licking Paulette's ear.

Paulette pulls away. What do you think I am, double-gaited?

> *A melody haunts my reverie*
> *and I am once again with you . . .*

Trotsky's mouth drops open as he watches Frida try to kiss Paulette.

> *. . . when our love was true . . .*

Diego smiles as he watches Trotsky watching Frida.

Aren't you tired of playing the little tourista, Frida asks.

Wherever I go, doors open for me, Paulette answers.

I'll open your door, Frida says, clasping Paulette tighter.

> *A nightengale sings his fairy tale . . .*

Do you mind? Trotsky asks, trying to cut in.

Yes I mind, Frida says.

Give me a chance to explain about Barcelona, he pleads.

Frida waltzes away with Paulette.

Trotsky stands there, his shoulders slump.

What are we looking at? Frank asks Sylvia. Heartbreak?

None of our business, Sylvia says.

Flecks of light cross the dancers and dissolve them into atoms.

They revolve in their orbits around the glittering floor.

It is dancing, and it isn't about getting somewhere.

And it goes on.

FRIDA'S CREMATION

After Siqueiros, Cardeñas, and Rivera
guard her remains and the red flag on her coffin
After the slow cortege through the city
After pall-bearers place her on the conveyor-belt
After the funeral director ignited the gas-jets
After they leap to life like banked rows of blue shark's teeth gnashing
After the mortician throws the switch
Frida begins to sail head-first through the door of fire
A scorching wind roars out to singe Diego's face
Her sister Cristina rushes to snatch the rings off Frida's fingers
Diego's eyes dry out from staring
A pulse of silver light rushes through him
Frida's hair, blazing
He remembers the last entry in her diary
Feet, what need have I of feet when I have wings to fly?
Diego pulls a pencil from his vest pocket
He sketched her skeleton in his address book
Even her bones are beautiful
Her smile turns to ash

IV

Time is not a flow, but a pulsation.
—Philip Turetzky,
"Nietzsche: Eternal Return," from *TIME.*

INCIDENT ON CERILLOS ROAD

In red ink death writes
his usual script. An old man
bolts across a divided highway,
a white Buick kisses him at the knees.
He rises into the air as if
an albino bull with chrome horns
has hooked him. The last thing he learns
is how to fly. The sun makes
a gold spot on the tarmac. His broken legs
splay at crazed angles. Two by-standers
kneel to check his pulse.
Others near their cars
thumb the sign across both eyes.
To the stunned driver the angel who
holds the old man's head becomes
more visible as blood stains its feathers.
Police sirens part the common blare of day.
Medics pray on his chest with crossed hands.
His dead tongue, sticking out, relapsing in,
says *this, this.*

An Inmate at Utah State Prison Looks at Mt. Tippenoga

Far off east
under a storm's shroud
the icy mountain he will climb
when his stretch has all been served
calls from November silence.
He counts the million steps of rock
marked by bands of snow he will ascend —
one for each mistake.
He tells himself he's not afraid,
yet he knows his knees will buckle.
The steps will rise beyond the clouds.
How many times will he fall,
scattering cliff swallows,
bouncing like the rag doll of himself
before he has worked his questions out?
When he reaches the summit
a white dot from behind the moon
will swiftly grow until its angel wings
span from Mexico to Canada.
It will blow a breath into his lungs,
uncoil the placental rope.

Notes on Grace

Driving back east through cornfields,
cornfields under fluorescing skies
stalks with outreaching palms, receiving light,
turning it to life, what they are, how they're formed
perfectly together. The highway
loops up ramps and suddenly towers, in rows,
brick red, marble white, with mile-long
freight trains slow rolling through stockyards,
stockyards, steam, smoke, rising, making haze.
Come with me,
if you want to go to Kansas City,
I find myself singing out the car window
to Charlie Parker's ghost,
feeling him reach inside the fibres of song
to leap oxygen scales with night's blue statement —
So long, pretty baby,
the time has come for me to bid adieu
and the promised poetry of the road
becomes a sky filled with neon
Put a twenty dollar gold piece on my watch-chain ...
don't cry over me, 'cause I'm goin' to Kansas City.
An effortless movement of alto air,
corn leaves lifting in a rain-filled breeze.

LEARNING TO LISTEN

The difficulty begins in the fear
we will never be heard. But even
thunder rests from hill to hill. Step
by step, strangers in this retreat learn
to hear the silence between, the way
skaters pull each other into spins.
Memories spray up like razored ice.
Each day is sufficient to its story as
wild raspberries ripen through tone
after tone of red, and strangers learn
to walk the woods to what becomes
the usual delight of trout in ponds.
Out of sight, the sound of thoroughbreds
cantered breathless by stable jockeys
mixes with a melody from a piano,
as a composer somewhere in a cottage
finds, note by recursive note, the music
for this spectral place and a deeper way
to touch than touching.

SECOND WIND

I drove to where she used to live.
The house was empty, eyes shut.
I asked the mailman where she was.
She died, he said, her husband sold
the place. I sat in my car remembering
that photograph, the two of us climbing
my uncle's garden fence. Five-year-olds.
We played in the blackberry thickets.
When we stooped through their arches,
we were inside. I told her the story
my mother read, when Brer Rabbit said
'Don't throw me in that briar patch'
and she smiled under the roar of bombers
winging toward Tokyo
to the rumble of God's mill wheels
grinding daylight over green canopies.
She was the one I told my visions to.
But for a while we used to play war,
and when I said I'd been shot by a sniper
with palm frond camouflage in his helmet
high in bamboo elms, she would kneel
beside me with her blond pigtails, say
"tip-tock-a-lock" as she touched my chest
and send the shiver of life through me.

JOANNE

We were that age
when all you know is what you
don't want, before the drunken midnight
phone calls. We hung out
at the Uptown Diner. She jammed
quarters into the lit jukebox's right lung
and punched numbers. Little Richard
banging "Long Tall Sally" before
he got religion. The music rocked us like
orphans. As her music logic shifted
"Don't Be Cruel" after "In the Still of the Night."
As shoppers bent through sleet toward Christmas
words zagged through her cigarette lips.
She'd start in about her boyfriend, her eyes like
blown out umbrellas. She'd grip
the juke's shoulders as if to shake out
a song that would make a difference to a guy
whose father treated him like a human sacrifice
waiting for a bad holiday.
I got a gal named Boney Maroni,
        bah-bah bah-bah,
        bah-bah bah-bah bah-bah
She looks just like a stick of macaroni.
They say rock 'n roll djs invented the art
of stringing cuts together. It wasn't
them. It was Joanne, looking at me
with her earth angel eyes, You're a man,
she said. You can leave. No, I couldn't.

THE UNDEAD

We are the undead,
the shoot 'em-in-the-head dead
our tombstone faces smeared with mire.
Ho-he-ho, we intone as we groan
to work on the freeway like a chorus of feathered
tag-team wrestlers in sequined hardhats
getting ready to rumble
to make the world safe for the vitally-challenged.
Disturbing signs have appeared
in the western sky, rumors of women
teaching their children to fly, teenagers playing
their loud whatever music in
our air-space. No one has to order us
to leave our graves and stumble
like an army of blind witch-wanders
toward those of you living in ranch houses
on the edge of town. We don't know
why you're so afraid of us.
We pay our taxes, obey the laws
of circumstance. It's this urge to surge
into your dens and channel surf on the cable
Mummy Network for our favorite shows:
Mausoleums of the Rich and Famous,
Interesting Test Patterns, the Home Funeral Hour.

AUTO-DE-FÉ DREAM

A black mist hisses under highway Michelins.
Mascara-heavy eyes squint windshields
squeak kaleidoscope wipers.
Homeward the real estate women
in their big silk bows, worklife harried
and cursing, flipping each other dirty birds,
lane-surfing, tail-gating, hitting brakes,
blurred crimson treads slash on tarmac,
horns shanking winter evening air,
Yuletide mall music cranked to lethal.
The eye in the sky 'copter hovers as two
suburban assault vehicles hump to a stop
on an off-ramp, one high-heeled lady clicks
over to another, blasting her face
with a glove-box Glock 9. As the woman's soul
rises, pulled from her flesh like wet kleenex,
rivers of diamond-lit grids, tentacular beltways
resound with kettle-drum gunshots on clover-leafs,
vignettes of murder like a painting by Bosch
as all of us who took assertiveness training
eliminate the competition. At home
our orphans cache pipe-bombs, machine-guns
and take the revenge they feel entitled to.

BURIED TENOR

An infant is born without a soul
And there have been murders, cover-ups
Everyone knows, but turns away —
it's just too upsetting — we forego reparations
Nothing makes sense — *Because* disappears
and and permanently replaces *so*
A plethora of conflicting stories makes denial plausible
And everything in print is said to be law
We couldn't live with ourselves
if the Devil didn't make us do it
The author is dead, had to be killed
And she was the only one who could've told the story
Expressed the outrage, felt the desperation
Lifted our eyes in awe, rescued mystery from mystification
But narrative is now considered poison
And to hunger, to thirst for meaning's sake
Is to be a fascist now
Every poet's body burnt beside the bunker
And those who go on trying to make sense are down on their knees
Riding the vehicle, looking for the buried tenor
Making up alien abductions, cattle mutilations, black helicopters —
Sick with how boring it all is
Who did what when for whose benefit, huh?
Who cares? Buzz off angels!
No play on words, all there is is phantom pain
The amputated voice crashing into a Cosmic *Duh*

BLIND SIDE

One October morning
half my world goes missing
and in its stead a præternatural dark
like a church without a faith.
A midnight wraith paints one window
gray. What remains is a sentence
with no verb like the stanchions of a
bridge with no bridge. Of all I take for
granted, my body is the chief. My
mind's still good, I tell myself,
but chairs invisible in
corridors reach out to trip me.
Shinbarked, I totter. When I clutch
at walls to right myself I touch life's
cold edge. A pin rings
angelus on my optic nerve. No
surprise, no surprise. The light's half
gone, and what has changed?
The world is all surmise. Quicksand
or *terra firma*, I take my steps uncertain.
Hope still shapes what I imagine.

Redbrick Factory Blues

Hunched men with graveyard-shift eyes
wolfed fried potatos and chops under spinning blue neon
beer planets n all-night diners,
then dragged their bones to bed
watching moonlight carve angel cloud faces
as leaves lifted in unreachable
pre-dawn treetop breezes.
Nothing so sticky as dog day night.
They let their war-weary minds float out
on bar-room jukebox waves
listening to Patsy Cline strop her razor of love,
her voice reaching from laundry to jailhouse
where gristled drunks snored on chain-hung bunks
to tenements where rhinoceros uncles
punched holes in plaster walls
through wallpaper layers covered with yellow
nicotine film of smoking families
as the men imagined her, brushing her hair at a mirror
singing about loving — not a bad man
but one sick with gambling, whiskey, whatever
delirium he believed would lift him out of
fifty years of hard time, disspell
the nightmare of foreman ghouls breaking his spirit,
dancing on his grave. I *fall to pieces*, she sang
as absinthe violins pulsed in her veins.

OLD GIRLFRIEND DREAM

We meet in a very public place
a crowded mall cafeteria. Bright
display windows and mirrors. She
has, of course, a manuscript thick
with blue pages, all hand written.
I begin to read the way I do, last
one first, hit-or-miss, skipping here
and there. She has ink drawings
on every other page, a Cape Cod
beach, a boy buried in the sand.
None of this is about me, is it? I
ask. Remember, she says, how we
used to walk home from Notre Dame
dances, me listening as you told me
your dreams of one day writing
something great? She looks at me.
She hasn't aged a day, so shining
I avert my eyes to her colorful free
form assemblages. She has done
what I gushed about, not with her
life, but with life itself. When I hug
her I say my wife's name. Always
with you the mixed metaphors,
she laughs as she kisses me off.

TINY TIM AS I REMEMBER HIM

Tiny Tim waddles to center-stage
the Harpo Marx of pre-war '60s
with angel ringlets and cheap ukulele
and big snozzola who paid no payola
singing lays of gentler days in terza
rima, karma do, his spindly legs
are flying things with pointy wings
that barely bound along the ground
dip dough drew da dewlips wit chew
when Ed Sullivan was god, nothing
changed, always the same goofy acts
rearranged, Chinese jugglers spinning
plates with sticks and talking dogs
delivering long comic monologues
as others took to the streets wearing
white sheets or sarongs with bongs
blowing smoke up Miss Vicki
and others died in Mississippi to
pay everyone's dues to Mr. Blues
while Bob Dylan, heir to Walt Whitman
waited in the wings, tuning his strings.

American Fable

The grasshopper sawed
summer to dust with his fiddle,
playing the tune in his elbow's rivet.
The ant gleaned sunflower seeds
under the anvil's augury,
the season no game but salvation
by sweat, rumors of trades, bad mouths
in the dugout. Still the ant worked
as the grasshopper played pepper with sound,
his music a tool of constant surprise,
astounded by pop-ups, passed balls,
each run unearned,
making the ant's labors lighten by tons.
It was all manna to the fiddler,
a found corndog, a song out of thwaps,
a split-fingered grace. *Those who do not work
shall not eat,* the ant kept threatening,
until October frosted his metal eye
and the foolish fiddler
kept on singing *Blessed are those who swing
for they shall not be left like a house
by the side of the road,*
the sweet of the bat black with pine tar
going yard, its one wing opening
toward the constellation Grasshopper.

USES OF THE SLOW FADE

The world is in your face today —
every day, it seems — on the news
a woman is executed in Texas
and all you can think of as you
slump on your sofa after work
is how your mother used to call
you by your three names when
she was at her wit's end. You work
where homeless men gather in twos
and threes, the gray stain of hunger
on their skin, bedrolls on their backs.
Police make you just as nervous
as they. Because of them you keep
driving, past locust trees in the park,
giving off a silver light. What you
lay down they pick up. Your soul
is stretched like lycra webs whose
threads attach to long ago heart hooks.
All you can think of is how you're
lucky to live in a town with a river,
a little something going all the time.
You thank the garden wind that spins
the wings of your wooden flamingo,
thank the mercy of the slow fade.

A Juniper

Its flat branches seem rooted in the sky.
In broken granite, all gneiss and marl
it cypresses up into a snowless morning haze.
It seems odd, as if it were not a native
but blown here from some distant coast
like Carmel, Monterey,
a ghost ship run aground,
a shrine whose spars turn like twining cords,
to writhe its capillaries deep into the earth,
and though it's hacked with machetes
by people with no respect
it has all the more character
having survived,
shaking in the western mountain breezes
where the Chinook comes
eating ground snow with desert teeth,
all 144 of its ears pointed to
where yucca bells stand
above the Poudre River's liquid song
knit with killdeer cries.

WALKING TO ROUND BUTTE

When my friend and I start off
down mud wheelruts in the county
easement the wind begins to shrill
through patches of buffalo grass
carved like brain coral. He's crossed
this range before and finds a parchment
puffball, perfectly round, a half-inch
across at its bulging equator. I inspect
the narrow opening at its top. It's like
Acoma pottery, I observe, asking
 how he can find such small things.
Who knows, he says,
perhaps it's the original such seedpots
have been thrown from for centuries?
I ask how he does it. He says,
In midwinter on the high prairies
when it hasn't snowed, patches of
buffalo grass and angelwing cactus
tipped with rose quartz fruit form
regular shapes against which thumbs
of flint stand out. Red sandstone dust
is part of a background the eyes
grow used to. Here, where white sand
humps up, there's reason to suspect
an unmarked grave. So scanned
the land yields whatever stands out
as foreground to the land's common

weave like a Navajo blanket with one
telling flaw. Wind suddenly whistles
almost a song. A boulder you've been
guiding yourself by bounds off
changing itself into a striped antelope
that becomes yours. What anyone
finds — an arrowhead like a finger of
ochre fire, a smoky chip of obsidian
used to scrape fat off hides — becomes
a separate crossing. You might find
a rusted buckboard spring, and I
a small Stonehendge left from some
lineshack burnt to its foundation
a hundred years ago, outhouse and all,
besotted, he says with a grin, by ghosts
of cowboys who could spread apart
buffalo grass with chapped hands
and tell how many beeves might thrive
per acre. And, as we walk back to his
pickup, the flash in my old friend's eyes
sticks like milkweed in barbwire.

A FRONT RANGE SKY

From kitchen windows gold
sunset pastured horses drink and graze,
raising their body heat
for the coming January night.
Cottonwoods stunted by having
only the dirt road's spillover to
nourish them lie closer to the ground
than the well-fed. The wind
that makes their branches dance
in praise of the changing light
also drives an almost slate-colored
cloud the size of Rhode Island
over the foothills, buoying a smaller
cloud's flight, undulating its wings
like a manta ray, and beyond
like a company of steel guitars
other clouds scud west
out to pagodas of snow.
A polished aluminum sun
brightens as evening gathers
so bright time skips a beat.

SAMBA ON BASS AND ALTO

In the Santa Fe borders cafe with Jack
the melody begins, *I want to be loved,*
with inspiration, Cynthia and I the words
in our heads on our lips, the jazz duet's
fingers dipping, soaring through octaves,
the bassist with goatee, moustache, shock of
Beethoven hair, and I feel my blood
quick with old time Kerouac wine longings
for everything, as the lyrics take us
into arcs of solar heart flares, jagged
prayers ripping through why such distrust,
love not pure enough, closing throats,
as the bassist plucks like a mantis
in a rhapsody of claws, this music's appeal
I feel in my spiritside so heaped about
the everlasting, the bone man pumping his
sound cylinder, *I want to be loved,*
starting tonight, a flame, a fiddle throb
in tuxedo night. The sax says it's the only
flight between the plod-plod and edges for
anyone who's lived enough enoughs.

TRUSTING THE MUSIC

I can still hear his glasspack
bebop mufflers rumbling down Dead Horse Hill
in second gear, a wake of Bo Diddley
washing back over his primer-gray '51 Ford
top down like 47 miles of barbwire,
taking his first hit off a Lucky
like nothing could bust his chops
enough to silence the car radio that made us one,
him watching high school girls
with notebooks held shieldwise
over the tender mercies of their rosebuds,
not even paying attention to the road
but to the bandstand in his head
where he in a cobra-snake for a necktie
twanged chords that sent spasms through us
and we jumped up dancing.
He was the seventh son of the seventh son,
our Jean L'Conquereaux.
He had sat under a sumac tree
until he felt its branches pulse milk
down to something glowing beneath the roots
he held like a live coaxial cable
plugged into his guitar.

THE MUSIC WHILE THE MUSIC LASTS

Seventeen, wandering, drunk into
Greenwich Village strip joint ga-ga
at this boa constrictor worning its
way into a nearly naked woman's
g-string onstage. A b-girl grabbed
my ass. I though it was me, you
know, the girl couldn't help herself
and the word was about me. So
later when I fell by the Vanguard
this trumpet player was slow blues
like "*be*-bop," he was saying, mini-
mally, "*be*-bop," then chording up,
"*be*-bop," then down, "*be*-bop" with
a sad albeit gold horn. I snapped my
fingers at the bar. Two black guys
like NFL tackles glared at me to stop
popping. "Miles," the MC shouted,
making the *come-come applause
gesture*. This was 1958. Yesterday.
Charley Parker was dead. Even later,
when I started to listen, I heard Miles
was in his "Kinda Blue" period as
if it were not joy but Bird's horror of
silence that made him fill each bar
with 32nd notes. This was somehow
why the great soul of night was gone,
leaving a hole the size of Kansas City

in Miles. He was telling the story of
how Charley one night at Birdland
when people were clinking, chattering
he lost it, jumped off the bandstand,
put his fist through glass for a fire axe,
wading like Samson with the jawbone
of an ass into the Philistines, that they
would use him that way — as background
for their deals — creating a new
connotation for the word "axe." Only
later did I begin to dream poems could
be like that, new connotations spoken
when we stagger, struck by the beautiful
blunt instrument of the world.